Table of Contents

Kisah Hikayat Maryam Binti Imran Ibunda Nabi Isa AS Dan Burung Yang Tercipta Dari Tanah Liat

Edisi Bahasa Inggris

by

Jannah An-Nur Foundation

2020

While every precaution has been taken in the preparation of this book, the publisher assumes no responsibility for errors or omissions, or for damages resulting from the use of the information contained herein.

KISAH HIKAYAT MARYAM BINTI IMRAN IBUNDA NABI ISA AS DAN BURUNG YANG TERCIPTA DARI TANAH LIAT EDISI BAHASA INGGRIS

Prologue

Kisah Hikayat Maryam Binti Imran Ibunda Nabi Isa AS Dan Burung Yang Tercipta Dari Tanah Liat Dalam Bahasa Inggris Bersumberkan Dari Kitab Suci Al-Quran Serta Al-Hadist.

In the beginning I was clay then I became a bird by Allah's leave. From motionless clay to a soaring bird. I was something that was not able to move by itself and then I could fly in the sky. That is me.

I do not know how to introduce myself to history.

Allah SWT (Exalted and Glorified be He) introduced me in the last of His Books saying, "(Remember) when Allah will say (on the Day of Resurrection), 'O 'Isa (Jesus), son of Mary am (Mary)! Remember My Favor to you and to your mother when I supported you with Ruh-ul-Qudus [Jibril (Gabriel)) so that you spoke to the people in the cradle and in maturity; and when I taught you writing, Al-Hikmah (the power of understanding), the Tawrat (Torah) and the Injil (Gospel); and when you made out of the clay, as it were, the figure of a bird, by My Permission, and you breathed into it, and it became a bird by My Permission.'"(The Noble Quran)

That is me.

A handful of clay...I was the princess of clay, even though I was made of clay.

Then I fell in love. That was before Prophet Isa AS (Jesus) the son of Maryam (Mary) touched me. When I fell in love I began to transform.

How can a creature explain the scent of the earth that was originally the sky?

I was calm, still and content with my state of being a lump of clay. I do not dream, for clay does not have the ability to do this. Even though I could not dream, I was content. I had a long history before I became earthly clay. At first, I was a part of the sun. Then billions of years passed by and I had not yet fallen in love, so the burning embers were put out and I was transformed into rock on a planet they call the earth in a place they call Palestine The Land of Al-Aqsha Mosque.

Episode 1

{(Remember) when Allah SWT (God) will say on the Day of Resurrection, 'O 'Isa (Jesus), son of Maryam (Mary)! Remember My Favor to you and to your mother when I supported you with Ruh-ul-Qudus [Jibril (Gabriel)) so that you spoke to the people in the cradle and in maturity; and when I taught you writing, Al-Hikmah (the power of understanding), the Tawrat (Torah) and the Injil (Gospel),. and when you made out of the clay, as it were, the figure of a bird, by My permission, and you breathed into it, and it became a bird by My Permission.'} (AI-Ma'idah: 110)

In the beginning I was clay then I became a bird by Allah's leave. From motionless clay to a soaring bird. I was something that was not able to move by itself and then I could fly in the sky. That is me.

I do not know how to introduce myself to history.

Allah SWT (Exalted and Glorified be He) introduced me in the last of His Books saying, "(Remember) when Allah will say (on the Day of Resurrection), 'O 'Isa (Jesus), son of Mary am (Mary)! Remember My Favor to you and to your mother when I supported you with Ruh-ul-Qudus [Jibril (Gabriel)) so that you spoke to the people in the cradle and in maturity; and when I taught you writing, Al-Hikmah (the power of understanding), the Tawrat (Torah) and the Injil (Gospel); and when you made out of the clay, as it were, the figure of a bird, by My Permission, and you breathed into it, and it became a bird by My Permission.'"

That is me.

A handful of clay...I was the princess of clay, even though I was made of clay.

Then I fell in love. That was before Prophet Isa AS (Jesus) the son of Maryam (Mary) touched me. When I fell in love I began to transform.

Episode 2

How can a creature explain the scent of the earth that was originally the sky?

I was calm, still and content with my state of being a lump of clay. I do not dream, for clay does not have the ability to do this. Even though I could not dream, I was content. I had a long history before I became earthly clay. At first, I was a part of the sun. Then billions of years passed by and I had not yet fallen in love, so the burning embers were put out and I was transformed into rock on a planet they call the earth in a place they call Palestine The Land of Al-Aqsha Mosque.

I am a part of the mud of Palestine and a part of its land. Look how much I had suffered. Thousands of years passed by without falling in love.

I used to drink water, become satisfied and help scented flowers to grow even without enjoying love. It is the instinct of clay to be watered so we can grow flowers. One seed is enough for me to make what amazes both mind and heart. Through all this, I remained as I was, just simple earthly clay.

I did not see beyond the space taken by my atoms. Clay does not see with eyes for it does not have eyes. Sometimes I see things through a worm or a flower. I do not know what goes on around me; I do not know what happens on top of me. But, sometimes I feel happy and at other times I become sad.

The earth is sometimes happy and sometimes sad, even though it does not have a heart or feelings. Ah! This is one of the mysteries of clay and I do not know how to tell people about it. It is all right. I am not inclined to talk about myself but now I have the desire to do so. Is not a lover allowed to speak about his beloved?

When I fell in love, I, a simple piece of clay, fell in love with myself. I had heard about 'Isa before he was born. I saw him after he became a Prophet. Moreover, because of him I experienced the miracle of being transformed from clay into a soaring bird. I was a piece of clay in the garden that was right next to the Aqsa Mosque. On her way to prayer in the Mihrab (the place of worshiping), Maryam used to pass by me without stopping. I tried uselessly to get Maryam's attention but I could not. I gave it a lot of thought but I could not do anything.

Then one day a little rose bush grew from my mud. The bush was merely a green stem that had not yet turned dark green. I was surprised one day when Maryam stopped and looked at the rose bush. I tried hard to get her attention but I could not and amidst my confusion and sadness I sighed and a small bud opened in the bush.

Then, the virgin Maryam turned her face around and contemplated the miracle of the newly opened bud. That day Maryam watered me and the satisfaction I felt was different from the feeling I got when watered by rain. For, the water she watered me with, was the same water that she drank from. The water was sweet and scented with lemons and there was a heavenly taste to it. From that day forward, I never felt thirsty again. And I fell in love with Maryam. She was my first love.

For sure, a lover is allowed to speak about his beloved, isn't he?
I want to describe Maryam to you. O! I do not think that I
can, for I did not see her well. I just saw the part of her face
that was directly in front of me. Her face was pleasant and filled
with nobleness. Moreover, her eyes reflected a look that swayed
between the amazement of innocence and the beauty of pure
spontaneity. Her face was like a dream. It was like a flowing river.
Because I was unable to dream, I fell in love with her face twice.
Once because it is her face and once because I do not dream.
Even though I could not dream, my love for her was deep, calm
and silent.

"Ah! If only I possessed the bird's ability of expression. Ah! If
only I were a bird that could sing," I used to think in this way.

One day a bulbul stood on my mud and sang a short song that
sounded like a group of stars had joined together in cosmic
harmony. At that time I wished I were a bulbul to sing long at her
feet ...I mean at the feet of Maryam.

Among the wonders of love is that you do not know why you

fall in love. Then, your love increases and you. know why it
increases, while the original reason of falling in love, remains a
mysterious secret never to be revealed. So I did not know the
reason behind my love for Maryam. Then, one day my love for
her increased and I knew why,

"(And (remember) when the angels said, 'O Maryam (Mary)!
Verily, Allah has chosen you, purified you (from polytheism and
disbelief), and chosen you above the women of . the 'Alamin
(mankind and jinn) (of her lifetime).'"

I understood then that I fell in love with the one, whom Allah SWT (God) had crowned a princess from among the women of the worlds ... And I understood the reason for her purity that made the moon seem like a faded candle.

My love for Maryam increased ...For how could particles of mud resist falling in love with something of such value.

The angels once again addressed Maryam, "O Maryam! Submit yourself in obedience to your Lord (Allah, by worshiping none but Him Alone) and prostrate yourself; and Irka'i (bow down etc.) along with Ar-Raki'in (those who bow down etc.)."

Thus she was ordered after receiving the glad tidings to increase her submission to Allah, to prostrate to Allah, to bow down (in prayer) to Allah and to worship Him devoutly. I was happy on her behalf but sad for myself, for Maryam forgot me for a year as she became busy performing prayer. When Maryam prayed, the amount of universal nobleness increased and satanic disobedience and rebellion in comparison, seemed like a handful of ashes, whose flames have died out. Ah! Maryam forgot me for a long time. She was busy with prayer but I waited for her everyday. It was a kind of torture to wait. Moreover, I did not find anybody to complain to except the rosebush. The rosebush had now turned into a rose tree.

I said to the rose tree, "The virgin Maryam has forgotten us."

The rose tree did not say anything.

I again said, "Maybe she has not forgotten us."

Episode 3

The rose tree remained silent. The wind blew so that one of the roses moved and a drop of water fell from its white petals. I did not know if this was rain from the sky or if it was the rose crying ...I did not know. All I knew was that the drop of water was the only answer that the tree gave during our conversation.

At the same time, I imagined that Maryam cried while she was praying and I was filled with muddy conviction that Maryam's tears were what had made the rose cry. The amount of my love for Maryam increased as I waited for her; and increased as the rose tree grew. Moreover, it seems that love filled me with fertility that I never realized existed in me and so dozens of rose trees were born.

All of us waited for the Virgin. Then, one day a cosmic event occurred. The sun shone and dried up all my mud, and rain clouds passed over me without stopping. I cracked from thirst. However, my thirst to see the princess that Allah crowned upon all the women of the worlds was stronger than my thirst for water. Finally, the sun descended towards its mysterious bed in the west and night came. It was a hot summer's day and the thirst of the roses increased, and so the smallest one leaned towards me and said, "I am going to die of thirst. Should I start my journey towards wilting?"

When the rose asked me, I did not reply as I did not know what to say. I prayed a short prayer to Allah to save us from thirst. Before I finished my prayer, Maryam ran towards me holding a jug of water that was spilling as she hurried. Maryam remembered me suddenly after her prayer, and so she came just at the right moment. Maryam watered me and I silently drank the water then pushed it towards the stems of my bushes and made sure that they drank.

Then, suddenly a great universal event occurred. I felt it when the angel's foot trod upon the ground. Jibril (the master of angels) descended and stood right in front of Maryam. I sensed his presence before Maryam even saw him. Actually, despite the fact that I am mere mud, we feel, sense and react to Allah's Miracles before humans do. When Jibril descended, the particles of my mud were filled with a desire to fly and the flowers raised their white heads and looked at him in wonder.

After a few moments, Maryam saw him. At first, she was surprised but when she gazed at his face she realized that she did not know him. For Jibril took the form of a human being but his splendor shone like a ray of light from his human disguise. Maryam felt scared, so she sought Allah's protection. She thought he was a strange man that had crept up upon her when she was alone.

Feeling afraid, she said, "Verily! I seek refuge with the Most Beneficent (Allah) from you, if you do fear Allah."

The Lord's angel Jibril smiled at her so as to put her fears to rest.

He quietly answered her, 'I am only a Messenger from your Lord."

When Maryam felt reassured, the Lord's angel told her why he had descended to the earth. He said, "(To announce) to you the gift of a righteous son."

Maryam became happy but her happiness was shattered before it even began. She remembered that she was a virgin. No human had touched her. She was not married ...How could she give birth?!

These thoughts flew through Maryam's head like scared birds.

She asked the Honest Spirit, "How can I have a son, when no man has touched me, nor am I unchaste?" He said, "So (it will be), your Lord said, 'That is easy for Me (Allah) and (We wish) to appoint him as a sign to mankind and a mercy from Us (Allah), and it is a matter (already) decreed, (by Allah).'"

In our worldly life, there are statements that carry great meaning and what Jibril said to Maryam that day is one of these phrases. He said to her, "It is a matter (already) decreed "

He wanted to put an end to a long discussion that would result from Maryam's astonishment after discovering that she would be pregnant and would give birth by Allah's Decree.

Maryam was a virgin who had been given as a servant to al-Aqsa Mosque by her family. It was her honor and glory that she was a virgin and at the service of al-Aqsa mosque. "How can a virgin give birth? What will people say? How will she be able to defend herself in an evil world that does not believe in Allah's Miracles or His Ability?" I thought.

Being a piece of mud I did not know what Maryam's feelings, worries or thoughts were. No one save Allah knew. That was why the Lord's angel told her, "It is a matter (already) decreed" He put an end to her fears or in other words, ordered her not to think about it as it was a matter already decreed by Allah.

So, Maryam's task then was to channel her thoughts and inquires towards something else. She had to surrender to the decreed matter. At that time Maryam had to surrender and be optimistic and happy, for Allah (Glorified and Exalted be He) has willed that she be purified and above the women of all the worlds, and has willed that she be the mother of a gracious Prophet by a Word from Allah.

The Lord's angel blew in the air and so the Miracle occurred and the virgin became a mother carrying a sign from Allah. "It is a matter (already) decreed."

Maryam repeated this sentence after the angel disappeared and then she ran fast towards her Mihrab forgetting the jug she had drunk from, that she came to water us with. I loved Maryam the virgin mother more than I loved Maryam the virgin. My love for her flourished with my love for the baby of Allah's Will.

Episode 4

Days and months passed by. I saw Maryam a lot. At a short distance from me there was a lot of tall palm trees and the virgin mother used to walk from the east spot where my mud lay to the palm trees that were only a few steps away. She used to stand for a long time at the palm trees or sit on the grass or praise Allah or remain silent and pale. Then, one day the pains of childbirth came to her while she was sitting next to the trunk of a palm tree.

She said amidst her pain, "Would that I had died before this, and had been forgotten and out of sight!"

Despite Maryam's tremendous faith, and despite Allah's Choice of her; and despite His Will that she carried His Signs to humans despite all this glory, the virgin had more cause to worry than to be reassured. This was simply human anxiety, that I understood very well. Maryam belonged to a human society not an angelic one. She was subjected to human laws. It is a part of these laws that a woman should not give birth except if she is married. So, if Maryam claimed that she did not get married and then gave birth, this would be a proof of her being unchaste.

That is no small and trivial problem. The virgin would be accused of being unchaste. What a sacrifice given by those humans who are chosen by Allah! The sacrifice in their case begins with honor, and then ends with their bodies being hammered with nails, sawed or stabbed treacherously from the back.

Maryam was the purest woman on the earth and despite that, her whole society repeated these words, "O sister (i.e. the like) of Harun (Aaron) [not the brother of Musa (Moses), but he was another pious man at the time of Maryam (Mary)]! Your father was not a man who used to commit adutery, nor your mother was an unchaste woman."

Maryam thought about this sentence before she gave birth and it tortured and astonished her, for she did not choose what had happened to her, but rather it was a matter already decreed by Allah. That was what the Lord's angel had told her.

When she felt the pains of child birth she uttered words of human weakness. She said, "Would that I had died before this, and had been forgotten and out of sight!"

What torture made her say these words! For sure, it was a torture that exceeded human capacity of endurance. On the outside it was a torture, but tender mercy and Divine Glory were at its core.

Maryam said those words while she was giving birth. She was surprised by the coming of the baby and saw in her mind what she would endure at the hands of the people of her society and as she thought about that, she returned to human weakness and wished that she was a thing forgotten and out of sight. At the same time, a voice cried out from beneath the palm-tree,

"Then [the babe 'Isa or Jibril] cried unto her from below her, saying, 'Grieve not! Your Lord has provided a water stream under you. And shake the trunk of date palm towards you, it will let fall fresh ripe-dates upon you. So eat and drink and be glad, and if you see any human being, say: Verily! I have vowed a fast unto the Most Beneficent (Allah) so I shall not speak to any human being this day.'"

The situation was over and the virgin's abstinence from talk began. She went out with the child and came back to her people carrying him. Then, the gossip started and the Jewish community talked about nothing except the virgin that had given birth. The evil of the Jewish community surpassed the incredible phenomenon of what had just happened. Their mouths were filled with mud that filled the atmosphere.

I represented the earth and my children, I mean the roses, represented plants ...and together we were witnesses to Maryam's chastity and innocence. We were not the only witnesses, for the whole universe was a witness to her innocence. Moreover, the Lord of the universe knows everything. Despite that, Maryam went through some hard times. Nevertheless, deep down the Jewish community knew that Maryam was innocent but its hypocrisy made it accuse her.

Even though I am just earthly mud, I can understand this strange phenomenon. When a certain society suffers from decadence, it refuses to believe that purity and chastity of any kind existed. Furthermore, this society itself stands against any kind of purity and chastity. When purity exists in its most elevated form, it hurts the feelings of hypocrisy and corruption ...and corruption therefore draws its weapons and wages war. No war is easier to wage than a war of debase gossip.

Then something occurred that should have put an end to the whole situation or was supposed to do that. However, this occurrence did not succeed in stopping the soiled tongues.

Maryam came back carrying 'Isa (peace be upon them) and her people asked the very same question that had gone through her mind when she wished that she was dead, "O sister of Harun (Aaron), Your father was not a man who used to commit adultery, nor your mother was an unchaste woman. "

She remembered what 'Isa said to her so she pointed to him. They understood that she had made a vow of silence, but now their astonishment increased. How could they talk to a child that was new born! The head of the priests said to Maryam, "How can we talk to one who is a child in the cradle?"

Then, the miracle happened and 'Isa talked! He said, "Verily! I am a slave of Allah. He has given me the Scripture and made me a Prophet. And He has made me blessed wheresoever I be, and has enjoined on me Salat (prayer), and Zakat, as long as I live. And dutiful to my mother, and made me not arrogant, unblest. And Salam (peace) be upon me the day I was born, and the day I die, and the day I shall be raised alive!

Despite this decisive miracle the war of gossip still circulated around Maryam, for the Jewish society continued telling this story after failing to mention the miracles in it. But, both my feeling of pain and my love for Maryam and 'Isa increased. In spite of the fact that I am mere mud and despite of my simple rank in the worldly life, I feel pain and love and also feel happy or sad.

Days passed by and I did not see Maryam anymore. Maryam forgot the jug in which she had brought us water. She forgot it in a place close by me. "O Allah! How can she drink then?" I thought. I missed hearing about Maryam and her great son.

Episode 5

Then, one day some guards of the Roman ruler Herod passed by me and with them was an investigator that seemed to be from the Intelligence Agency.

This man asked a lot of questions.

The man looked at the rose bushes, the vineyard and the palm trees. He ordered a table to be set up next to my ground and he sat and asked everyone, "What is the story of the child that talked in its infancy? What is the story of the gossip that says that he is the savior that will save his people? Who are his people? From whom will he save them? Will he save them from Rome? Is there a conspiracy against Rome? Will a baby still wrapped in a blanket lead this conspiracy? Is this baby just a cover for older men who are the planners of this conspiracy?

Who are they?"

The questions of the investigator showered upon the priests and friars of the temple and everyone who was in the market, as well as anyone who had heard, seen or even imagined that he had heard or seen something about it. It was obvious that the situation had irritated the Roman authorities. Moreover, the people realized that the state's hand was moving and about to strike. So, they hid the whole story and completely denied it.

One of the priests answered the investigator saying, "Do you believe sir, that a baby can be born without a father?" He answered the second question saying, "Do you believe sir, that an infant can talk?"

The investigator raised his head and said, "Priest, just answer my questions. I have not come here for you to ask me and I answer you."

The investigator's voice' suddenly became harsh. The priest felt scared of the investigator's harshness and said, "Mr. Investigator, you are asking me about illusions and dreams. I do not believe that a virgin gave birth and that her baby talked. No one believes this superstitious tale. They have bothered you sir without excuse."

The Roman investigator felt depressed that he left Rome and came to Palestine pursuing illusions. The Jewish priest's words convinced him for they were logically correct. The people heard about the investigator and told each other to completely hide the story of the Christ that was born by a Word of Allah, and who talked only moments after his birth. That was the safest thing to do due to the hard circumstances of that time. All the people denied what they had seen with their eyes and heard with their ears. The investigator was contented with the results, gathered his paperwork and returned to Rome.

The investigator disappeared and I did not see him again.

Episode 6

Two days after the disappearance of the investigator, Maryam appeared once again. She carried her son in her arms and walked in the darkness of the night. She stopped every few steps and looked around. The Lord's angel appeared to her and ordered her to travel to Egypt. She said she was afraid of traveling but the angel reassured her and explained to her that all the people who carry a message, leave their home for sometime.

In this way Maryam left and I did not know anything about her for years. I loved Egypt just as I loved Maryam and her son the miracle of Allah. I knew that Egypt's mud was tender to them and sheltered them and I felt that the land of Egypt loved them as much as I did.

Years passed by and the Jewish community reached the peak of its hypocrisy. There was a facade that they had to keep up and an inside reality that was' completely full of evil actions. The Law was strictly applied and injustice prevailed and became the law of life. There were seven levels to purity and twenty-six prayers that had to be said while washing hands before eating food. There was nobody that was pure in the whole society and prayer became mere rituals. The prayer had become devoid of its content, it had neither connection nor submission to Allah. Priests were being bribed and they distorted the Torah; they left a part in and took a part out. The priests sold sacrifices of birds and doves that would redeem people of their sins, as they falsely thought, for a lot of money and so became rich at the expense of the poor worshipers. A kind of intellectual bartering prevailed in society. The minds were corrupted and so were the bodies.

From the outside there was a kind of fanaticism in the way religious texts were applied and that was in turn met with a horrible looseness in the attention given to the soul of religion.

In this way the Jewish community's facade was made up of a human system that was completely worn out from the inside. The only value that was worshiped at that time was gold or money in general. The importance of the soul was cancelled from the dictionary of values to the extent that Jews thought that a creature's blood was his soul.

Prophet Isa AS was a human that came by a Word of Allah and His Spirit. The aim of his call was to elevate the Word of Allah and the spirit of the true religion.

All his miracles were connected to the soul. He gave life and death. Does this not revive the spirit of the one who died and prove the existence of the soul (or spirit) and the existence of resurrection? His miracle with me (the mud) was also connected to the soul. 'Isa (pbuh) wanted to destroy the concept of physical existence as a superior form of life. For this reason he fed thousands from just one fish. He wanted to tell people about the reality of the soul as it fills up the form of the body. This form does not become greedy except if it loses consciousness of the soul. If the soul fills the body, thousands could be satisfied by one fish.

Episode 7 Epilogue

Then, came my turn.

People think that if a person died and returned to the earth, it would be impossible to be resurrected. They thought that life was over, and the soul is lost with the blood and so all was gone.

People talked to 'Isa about this and he calmly listened to their ignorance. Then one day 'Isa sat next to the rose tree and a big crowd gathered around him. They talked to him about the soul and showed their suspicion of the value that 'Isa imagined about the soul. 'Isa looked around him then bent down to the ground and held a piece of clay that was me in his noble hands. I was raised from the ground for the first time in my life. 'Isa listened to what they said while he pressed me. I felt that his pressure filled me with something new. 'Isa raised the piece of clay in his hands and asked those around him, "What is this?"

The people replied, "This is a piece of earthly clay." 'Isa asked, "Can this piece of clay fly in the sky?"

They answered, "No! It cannot!"

He asked them why it could not, but they did not answer.

Prophet Isa AS (Jesus) explained, "Because it is void of soul. If I formed it into

a bird and blew into it asking Allah to put a soul in it, would it then not fly?" While 'Isa spoke he formed me into a bird and when he finished, he blew at my body and I turned into a bulbul and flew away looking at 'Isa and the crowd that had gathered around him. I started singing and I spread my wings and flew... What pleasure for one to be a bird that can fly up to the sky. 'Isa was talking as I was getting farther away. I will fly to Maryam (Mary). I want to sing at her feet for a long time. The scene was getting smaller each time I went higher in the sky.

O Ya Allah! I am getting higher and higher....

About the Author

"And give good tidings to those who believe and do righteous deeds that they will have gardens [in Jannah Paradise] beneath which rivers flow. Whenever they are provided with a provision of fruit therefrom, they will say, 'This is what we were provided with before.' And it is given to them in likeness. And they will have therein purified spouses, and they will abide therein eternally." (The Noble Quran 2:25)